The snow queen

Hannie Truijens

Illustrated by Joanna Troughton

Chapter 1   The broken mirror   page 3

Chapter 2   Gerda and Kai   page 5

Chapter 3   The magic flower garden   page 16

Chapter 4   The prince and the princess   page 21

Chapter 5   The little robber girl   page 24

Chapter 6   The ice palace   page 28

Nelson

Thomas Nelson and Sons Ltd
Nelson House Mayfield Road
Walton-on-Thames Surrey
KT12 5PL UK

Text © J. C. M. Truijens 1989
Illustrations © Macmillan Education Ltd 1989
This edition: illustrations © Thomas Nelson & Sons Ltd 1992
Illustrated by Joanna Troughton

First published by Macmillan Education Ltd 1989
ISBN 0-333-48473-8

This edition published by Thomas Nelson and Sons Ltd 1992

ISBN 0-17-400552-0
NPN 9 8 7

All rights reserved. No part of this publication may be reproduced,
copied or transmitted, save with written permission or in accordance
with the provisions of the Copyright, Design and Patents Act 1988, or
under the terms of any licence permitting limited copying issued by the
Copyright Licensing Agency, 90 Tottenham Court Road, London W1P 9HE.

Any person who does any unauthorised act in relation to this publication
may be liable to criminal prosecution and civil claims for damages.

Printed in China

Chapter 1: The broken mirror

One day an evil spirit made a magic mirror. This mirror made all good and beautiful things look ugly and wicked, and it made all evil and ugly things look good and lovely. The evil spirit was so pleased with his mirror that he went to show it to the good spirits.

The closer the evil spirit came to the good spirits, the more the mirror shook. At last the mirror shook so hard that it fell out of the evil spirit's hands.

The magic mirror fell down to the earth and broke into a million tiny pieces. The people who got a piece of the mirror in their eyes only looked for the bad things in the world. The people who got a piece of mirror in their hearts became cold and cruel. Their hearts turned to ice.

The evil spirit was so pleased with his work that he laughed until the sky rumbled.

Chapter 2: Gerda and Kai

Two poor children lived in the middle of the city. They lived next door to each other, in the attics of two houses, and they loved each other like a brother and sister.

There was no room in the city for gardens but the children were lucky. They shared a small roof garden with roses.

The girl's name was Gerda and the boy's name was Kai. In the summer they were often outside on the roof. In the winter they stayed inside and Kai's grandmother told them stories.

Kai's grandmother told them about the snow queen. "At night the snow queen flies through the streets of the city and looks in through the windows. Then the windows freeze and look as if they have big flowers on them."

One winter evening Kai was getting ready for bed. He looked out of the window and saw a big snowflake on the edge of the empty window box. It grew bigger and bigger and turned into a woman. It was the snow queen. She was very beautiful but as cold as ice. She waved to Kai and her eyes glittered like stars.

Kai ran to his bed. When he peered from under his blankets the snow queen had gone.

Soon it was spring again. The roses in the roof garden were lovelier than ever. Gerda and Kai loved the roses very much and made up a little song about them:

"The roses bloom and die,
But we will go to the Christmas child."

One day Kai and Gerda were sitting outside and looking at a picture book. Suddenly Kai felt a sharp prick in his heart and in his eye.

"Ow," said Kai, "that hurts." Gerda looked in his eye, but could see nothing. "I think it's gone," said Kai. But it wasn't gone. A small piece of the magic mirror had gone into Kai's heart and eye.

Gerda was sorry for Kai and had tears in her eyes.

"Why are you crying?" shouted Kai suddenly. "There's nothing wrong with YOU, is there? You look so ugly when you cry."

Gerda stared at Kai. She couldn't believe that he could be so unkind.

Kai ran to the roses. "They're ugly," he said, "and they have bugs on them." He pulled off the roses and kicked the flower box. He grabbed his picture book and went inside.

Gerda was very upset. Kai had suddenly changed. She couldn't understand it.

Gerda didn't know that the magic mirror was doing its work and that Kai's heart was growing colder and colder.

From that day on Kai didn't want to play with Gerda. When the winter came again he took his sled to the city park where all the big boys played. They tied their sleds to the farmers' waggons and rode along.

A very big sled came through the park. It was all white and the woman in the sled was dressed in white fur. Kai tied his sled to the big one.

The woman in the big sled nodded at Kai. It seemed as if she knew him. When Kai wanted to go home he tried to untie his rope but he couldn't get his sled loose. Suddenly they drove out of the city gates.

Kai was afraid and started to shout for help. Nobody heard him and the sled went faster and faster. Soon they were far away from the city.

At last the sled stopped. The woman in white stepped out and Kai saw that her fur coat and hat were made of snow. Then he knew who she was. "You must be cold," said the snow queen. "Come into my sled."

She put Kai in the sled beside her and covered him with her coat of snow. She kissed him on his forehead and Kai's heart, which was already half frozen, turned into a lump of ice.

They flew up to a big thundercloud and the wind roared around them. They flew over forests and lakes, over land and sea. The wolves howled below them and the crows croaked above them. Kai looked at the moon and was happy.

Chapter 3: The magic flower garden

Nobody knew where Kai had gone. They said that he must have fallen into the river and drowned. Gerda was very unhappy all winter long. In the spring she said to the sunshine, "Kai is dead and gone."

"I don't think so," said the sunshine.

"Kai is dead and gone," she said to the swallows.

"We don't think so," said the swallows. At last Gerda also believed that Kai was still alive.

One morning Gerda put on her new red shoes and went to the river to ask where Kai had gone. "Did you take my little friend?" asked Gerda. "I will give you my new red shoes if you will give him back to me."

It seemed to her that the waves nodded yes, so she threw her shoes into the water. The current brought them back to her. She stepped into a little boat to throw the shoes further into the river.

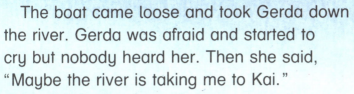

The boat came loose and took Gerda down the river. Gerda was afraid and started to cry but nobody heard her. Then she said, "Maybe the river is taking me to Kai."

The boat took Gerda past a lovely flower garden. An old woman with a big straw hat was working in the garden. Gerda shouted and the old woman pulled the boat in with a long hook.

Gerda told the old woman that she was looking for Kai. The old woman, who was a kind witch, didn't want Gerda to leave. She used her magic to make all the roses in her garden go under the ground. She knew that the roses would make Gerda think of Kai.

Gerda forgot about Kai, and spent the whole summer with the old woman. She loved the flower garden but it seemed to her that one kind of flower was missing.

One day Gerda was looking at the old woman's straw hat. It was decorated with flowers and the most beautiful one of all was a rose. The old woman had forgotten that she had a rose on her hat. Suddenly Gerda remembered Kai.

She asked all the flowers in the garden if they knew where Kai had gone. They all talked to her, but not one of them said a thing about Kai.

At last Gerda broke the rusty lock of the gate and left the magic garden. Outside the garden it was already autumn. "I have wasted so much time," cried Gerda. She walked until her bare feet were cold and sore.

Gerda walked and walked, and autumn turned into winter. She asked the trees and the bushes, she asked the rivers and the rocks, but they could not tell her where Kai had gone.

Chapter 4: The prince and the princess

Gerda sat down to rest in the snow. A big black crow hopped onto a branch in front of her. He greeted her and asked her why she was all alone in the cold wide world. Gerda told the crow about Kai and asked if he had seen him.

"Could be, could be," said the crow. "I think it was Kai, but I'm afraid he will have forgotten you. He is now married to a princess."

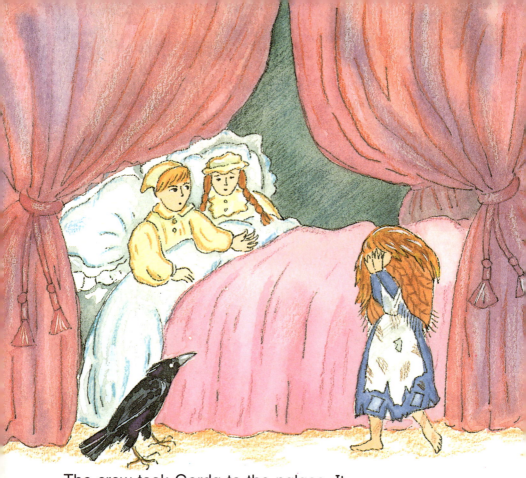

The crow took Gerda to the palace. It was night when they got there. They crept into the bedroom to look at the prince and princess. The princess was very beautiful, and the prince was very handsome, but he was not Kai.

Gerda started to cry. The prince and the princess woke up. "What's wrong?" they asked kindly. Gerda told them about Kai.

"You can stay with us," said the prince and the princess. "You will have everything you want."

"Thank you," said Gerda, "but all I want is to find Kai."

"Then we shall help you to find Kai," said the prince and princess. They gave Gerda new clothes, warm shoes and a coach, so that she could travel quickly. They helped her onto the coach and wished her luck.

Chapter 5: The little robber girl

The coach was made of gold and shone in the dark forest. A band of robbers saw the gold shining through the trees and rushed to attack it. They grabbed the reins and pulled Gerda down.

"She's nice and fat," said an old robber woman, "and will make a good meal." She pulled out a sharp knife but her daughter ran up to her and bit her in the ear.

"I want to play with her," said the little robber girl.

"Don't worry," she said to Gerda, "they won't kill you until I get bored with you. Are you a princess?"

"No," said Gerda, and she told the robber girl all about Kai and how much she missed him.

"What a lovely story," said the robber girl, "tell me again."

Gerda stayed with the robbers for a long time. Every night, before they went to sleep, the robber girl asked Gerda to tell her about Kai. The wild doves in the robbers' den also listened to her story.

One night the wild doves spoke to Gerda. "We have seen Kai," they said, "with the snow queen. They were going to the North Pole. Ask the reindeer where the North Pole is."

The next day Gerda told the robber girl what the doves had said. The robber girl said, "Well then, go and find your Kai. All the robbers are out and my old mother is still sleeping. Take my reindeer, he knows the way."

She gave Gerda some food for the journey, gave the reindeer a hard slap, and told him to take Gerda to the North Pole as fast as he could.

Chapter 6: The ice palace

They travelled for three days and then they were at the North Pole. They could see the palace of the snow queen from afar. It was made of ice and had a hundred rooms.

The reindeer took Gerda to the gates of the palace. He wouldn't go inside with her, but promised to wait for her outside.

Gerda stood alone in front of the ice palace. Snow monsters flew around her head and she was very frightened. Gerda thought of Kai and the roses and the snow monsters went away.

The snow queen had gone away. She was in another part of the world, making snow and ice. Kai was alone in the ice palace making an ice puzzle. He looked up coldly at Gerda when she ran inside.

"Kai, Kai, at last I have found you," cried Gerda. She kissed him and her hot tears fell on him. They melted his icy heart and washed the piece of magic mirror out of it.

Then Kai also started to cry and his tears washed the piece of mirror out of his eye.

"Oh Gerda," he cried, "I am so happy to see you. I'm sorry that I was so unkind to you."

"It doesn't matter," said Gerda. "I have come to take you home. Let's go quickly, before the snow queen comes back."

Gerda and Kai ran out of the ice palace to the waiting reindeer.

They rode on the back of the reindeer for three days. Gerda told Kai about all her adventures on the way. She told him about the magic garden, the prince, the princess, the golden coach and the robber girl.

Then they said goodbye to the reindeer and started the long walk home.

On the way they met the robber girl in the golden coach. She scolded Kai, kissed Gerda, and waved them goodbye.

Gerda and Kai walked past the magic garden. "I have found Kai," said Gerda to the old woman, "and we are going home."

The sun shone down on Kai and Gerda.

"I have found Kai," said Gerda to the sunshine, "and we are going home."

The swallows started to come back.

"I have found Kai," said Gerda to the swallows, "and we are going home."

When Kai and Gerda came home at last it was summer and their roses were blooming.